The Legend of the
Three Kings

© 2018 Simon Webb.

The right of Simon Webb to be identified as the Author of the Work has been asserted by him in accordance with the Copyright, Designs and Patents Act 1988.

The cover shows a study of a man in a turban, by Rubens (Getty Museum)

Except for the photograph on page 6, all other pictures are from the collections of the Getty Museum:

www.getty.edu

The Legend of the
Three Kings
by
John of Hildesheim
in a
Modern English Version
by
Simon Webb

Also from the Langley Press

An African Testament:
The Heart of the Kebra Nagast
in a Modern English Version

The Legend of St Alban

The Legend of St Cuthbert

In Search of the Northern Saints

The Voyage of St Brendan

The Life and Legend of Nicholas Flamel

What Do We Know About Pontius Pilate?

For free downloads and more from the Langley Press, please visit our website at:

http://tinyurl.com/lpdirect

Contents

Introduction	7
Preface	21
Prophecy	22
Nativity	29
A Journey	34
An Arrival	42
A Return	47
The Flight Into Egypt	50
St Thomas the Apostle	53
The End of the Three Kings	56
St Helen	59
More Travels	63
Devotion	65
The Opening of the Book in Middle English	71
The Wise Men, Matthew 2:1-12	72
Bibliography	73

Frederick Barbarossa, statue by H. Toberent, photo by H.U. Schmitt

Introduction

In 1160 the German Emperor Frederick Barbarossa started to besiege Milan, for the second time in three years. On the first occasion, in 1158, the siege had been concluded with a treaty before much harm could be done. The second time, it was no more Mr Nice Guy.

The siege Frederick started in 1160 dragged on until 1162, and there was disease, starvation and brutality on both sides. As if to give the Milanese a sense of his feelings about them, at one point during the final year of the siege Frederick returned six Milanese prisoners: five of them had been blinded as per his instructions, and the sixth had had his nose cut off. The noseless man had been allowed to keep his eyes so that he would be able to lead the others home.

When the desperate Milanese finally agreed to an unconditional surrender, the city fathers appeared before Frederick with their swords hung round their necks as a sign of their total subjection. Later, hundreds of Milanese prostrated themselves before the Emperor, begging for mercy. On the thirteenth of March, the emperor had the city evacuated, and ordered its demolition.

The tactic of dismantling an entire town or city at the end of a victorious siege was not uncommon in twelfth century Europe. Usually, churches and chapels were left standing, but the theory was that if there was no viable settlement, then there was no town or city for an enemy to re-take. The Milanese themselves had previously used this approach against the Italian city of Lodi, which was why people from Lodi allied themselves with Frederick in the fight against Milan.

The Emperor had entered Italy with too small a force to do anything like the damage he did, without help from Italian allies like the citizens of Lodi. These local allies were all too keen to help with the demolition of Milan, and they did not even spare the churches. Frederick himself had to intervene to stop some of the destruction, to allow certain precious items to be looted.

Among the greatest treasures of the Milanese were the supposed bodies of the Magi, or Three Kings, who had visited Jesus Christ in Bethlehem shortly after his birth. According to one story, the Milanese had concealed these relics in a bell-tower to prevent their falling into German hands. John of Hildesheim, author of the fourteenth-century *History of the Three Kings of Cologne*, tells us another story. According to him, the Milanese *buried* the bodies so that they would escape the looters. The location of the hiding-place was, however, revealed by a local man called Asso, who spilled the beans to avoid execution as an old enemy of Frederick Barbarossa. John of Hildesheim, a German monk, also explains in his book how the Three Kings had ended up in Milan in the first place.

It was perhaps inevitable that the Germans would take the Three Kings to their ancient city of Cologne. One of Frederick's closest advisers at this time was Rainald of Dassel, Archbishop of Cologne. Rainald brought the relics back to his city in triumph, and they were eventually installed in a sarcophagus which counts as one of the most gorgeous objects to have survived from medieval times. The celebrated shrine of the Three Kings, completed around 1225, ingeniously combines three coffins into a shape reminiscent of the nave of a church of the 'basilica' type. The shrine was made of wood and completely smothered with gold, silver, jewels and other decorations. The German King Otto IV donated golden crowns for the Three Kings in 1199.

A gold bust of Archbishop Rainald, who brought the Three Kings from Milan to Cologne, features as one of the decorations on their shrine in Cologne Cathedral. In this portrait, Rainald looks less like an archbishop and more like a king, with a gleaming, manly beard. This surely reflects his true character, and the niche he had carved for himself in life and history. He was certainly not a pious prelate who whispered in the Emperor's ear about the Prince of Peace and the brotherhood of man. On the contrary, he was a warmonger who may even have been personally responsible for scuppering a peace deal between the Germans and the Milanese, and extending the already tragically long siege of the Italian city.

Since they were perceived as holy monarchs, the Three Kings enjoyed a special status in the Europe of Rainald's time. The link between monarchy and religion is still evident in Britain, where the Queen is head of the Church of England, and is described on our coins as 'defender of the faith'. Modern British feelings about the religious role of the Queen do not, however, go as deep as those entertained on the subject of monarchy and Christianity in medieval Europe. Monarchs were seen as agents of God Himself, chosen by God and directly responsible to Him. Rebellion against a properly anointed monarch could be seen as a kind of sacrilege or heresy, and it is clear that rulers like Frederick Barbarossa tried to encourage this view of monarchy as a way of justifying their positions and their actions.

A manifestation of these religious feelings about monarchs – feelings that are hard to understand today – can be seen in the large number of royal saints that were revered in the Middle Ages. In England these included St Oswald, the saintly seventh-century king of Northumbria, and St Edmund, who perished at the hands of the Vikings in 869. St Edward the Confessor, who died in the memorable year of 1066, is also said to have been remarkable pure and pious. It is entirely typical that the cult of the martyred King Edmund should have been promoted by his younger contemporary, King Alfred the Great.

The elaborate appearance of the eleventh-century shrine of the Three Kings, that can still be seen in Cologne Cathedral, is a useful metaphor for the way the story of these early visitors to Jesus has been embroidered over the centuries.

Readers looking for the Three Kings in a typical English translation of the Gospels will not find any such personages. In Matthew, the only Gospel which mentions them, they are identified as 'Magi' or 'Wise Men', not as kings at all. Matthew hardly has space for much more information – the whole section on the Magi at the start of his second chapter comes to twelve verses and under three hundred words in the English version given in full at the end of this book. Many of these words are concerned with King Herod, his advisers and their advice to Herod about the likelihood that a Messiah figure might be born in a place called Bethlehem.

Matthew does not even tell us how many Magi there were. They gave three gifts, but that does not mean that there were three Magi. A close reading of the passage reveals that the Magi may not even have brought their gifts deliberately. They open 'their treasures' and offer Jesus gold, frankincense and myrrh, but we are not told that they deliberately bought or picked these out as gifts at home or during their journey.

Exactly where 'home' was for these men, however many there were of them, is also a mystery. Matthew tells us that they were from 'the east', but *where* exactly in the east does he mean? As John of Hildesheim makes clear in his book, it is quite possible that the Magi (whom he calls kings) did not all set out from the same place: John has them begin their journeys separately, then converge at no less a place than Calvary.

Various commentators, most of whom assume that the Magi set out together from the same place, have speculated about exactly where these mysterious easterners came from. In his 2017 book *Mystery of the Magi*, Dwight Longenecker insists that they must have come from Nabatea, an ancient kingdom the capital of which was Petra, the legendary rock-cut 'rose red city' which is now the top tourist destination in the modern state of Jordan. Longenecker's theory is just one of a number that place the home of the Magi somewhere in Arabia or the Syrian desert. Some of these theories rely on the nature of the Magi's gifts – all items that could be found in those places.

Others have taken the word 'magi' to suggest a link with the Zoroastrian religion, which was associated with Iran. If this is true, then we know both the geographical origin of the Magi, and their religion; but others have pointed out that various types of magi also flourished in Nebuchadnezzar's Babylonian kingdom (see R.E. Brown, *The Birth of the Messiah*, p. 167). The possibility that Matthew's Magi were Jewish astrologers from Babylon, who had gone against their religion and culture by embracing that profession, is also examined by Raymond Brown.

Whether the Magi came from Arabia, the Syrian desert, Babylon, Iran or elsewhere, the star that is associated with their journey west has also been the inspiration for some interesting theories. In his 1999 book *The Star of Bethlehem*, the astronomer Michael Molnar dismisses the possibility that the Magi's star was a nova or 'exploding star' because it seems that the astrologers of the first century were not interested in those at all. Molnar also makes short work of the theory that the star of Bethlehem was a comet: these were regarded as heralds of disaster, and were not associated with joyful events such as the coming of a wonderful new king.

Molnar sets out the case for Jupiter as the Magi's star: the planet was then associated with divinity and kingship, and it could have appeared to reverse its course in the sky in such a way that the Magi got the impression that it was stopping over Bethlehem.

While modern commentators try to strip away centuries of dubious accretions from the Magi story, make use of history and archaeology, and even apply the techniques of sciences such as astronomy to these New Testament characters, John of

Hildesheim, writing in fourteenth-century Germany, was apparently concerned to include as much material as he could in his account of the Three Kings. As he himself tells us, he drew his ideas from a wide range of sources, both written and oral. Where his sources seem to contradict each other, he will sometimes include accounts from both, then step back from his narrative and comment on their relative merits.

Whether John of Hildesheim actually believed that most of what he set down was true is an interesting question. If he personally did not believe most of it, then it may be that, like a modern folklorist, he was merely collecting legends; or was he compiling fantastical stories simply to entertain his readers?

The idea of John of Hildesheim as a medieval Baron Munchausen, deliberately spinning unlikely tales, is in line with at least one distinguished opinion of his *Three Kings*. John's book was 'discovered' by no less a person than Johann Wolfgang von Goethe, the colossus of German literature, who bestrode the eighteenth and nineteenth centuries, wrote *Faust*, applied his genius to many areas of the arts and sciences, and even dared to disagree with Isaac Newton.

The so-called Sage of Weimar wrote of John's book that:

> ... this little book belongs firmly in the tradition of the *Volksbuecher*, as it was invented and composed for humble people who enjoy uncritically whatever is offered to their imagination in a pleasing way. The details are indeed entirely delightful and have been embellished with a merry brush.

(trans. Dr C. Brown)

The German term 'Volksbuecher' has no precise equivalent in English: these were books of folk-tales or 'chapbooks', 'composed', as Goethe says, 'for humble people'.

Goethe was writing about a German version of John's book: John's own Latin original was probably intended for clerics, fellow monks, and perhaps monastic novices, rather than the local peasantry. Although John tells us that some of the materials for his book came from what we would now call oral tradition, he also cites and relies on a number of written sources, which suggests an attractive picture of the author using volumes from his monastery's library, but also recalling things he had heard.

As a friar, John of Hildesheim would probably have been out and about more than some medieval monks, who stuck strictly to their cloisters. The author may even have taught the theology and history he wrote about, which may have given him an idea of the kind of material that could catch and retain the attention of his listeners.

If John was aiming to tickle the uncritical imaginations of 'humble' readers and listeners with merrily embellished fantasy, then his choice of subject was well-suited to the purpose. Almost by definition, his narrative about the Three Kings has to spend a lot of time in 'the east', a vaguely-defined area which has served as a happy hunting-ground for the European imagination for centuries.

It may be that the exotic eastern flavour of much of John's *History* has something to do with the origins of the author's own monastic order, the Carmelites. The order may have been founded late in the twelfth century by a Norman French crusader who came to be known as St Berthold. The order derives its name from Mount Carmel in what is now the state of Israel, where Berthold is said to have organised a group of hermits into an order dedicated to the Virgin Mary. As well as its excessive praise for the Three Kings, John's *History* is also very complimentary about Mary, and provides many fascinating details about her life that cannot be found in the New Testament. According to John of Hildesheim, at one time God's mother had a garden in Egypt with several miraculous features, and had a tendency to leave her property behind during her travels in a way that benefited future generations of relic-hunters. These and other details make John's extensive treatment of Mary contrast with the brevity of his occasional cursory glances at her husband.

In his treatment of Mary and the Three Kings, John of Hildesheim includes many details about the places these people visited, and the condition they were in in the fourteenth century, when he was writing. As in his account of how Mary's Egyptian garden was faring under a Muslim sultan, some of the places John describes are just as fabulous as the events he relates.

Some of the most outlandish stories about 'the east' which engaged the medieval European mind were centred around Prester John, a legendary Christian priest-king ('Prester' means 'Presbyter') who ruled a large area of 'the east'. John of Hildesheim includes Prester John in his book, explaining that 'Prester John' was not really the name of a man, more a job-title held by a succession of Prester Johns.

The Prester John stories first seem to have made themselves known during the same century which also saw the looting of the bodies of the Three Kings from Milan, and perhaps the founding of the Carmelites. It is said that in 1165 Prester John sent identical letters to various rulers in Europe, setting out his stall as the mighty and pious ruler of rich and exotic lands. The letter stated that no less than seventy-two kings paid tribute to Prester John, and that within his wide empire there were creatures such as griffins, centaurs, fauns, satyrs, the phoenix, wild men, men with horns, men with just one eye, men with eyes pointing both forwards and backwards, and human cannibals.

Also in his supposed letter, Prester John stated that the cannibals, who did not fear death, were a great asset to him in times of war, since they cleaned up the battle-field by eating the dead, once he had given them permission to do so. Presumably Prester John had to fight wars from time to time to keep enemy nations away from the plentiful gem-stones of every type that were found in his dominions, along with other treasures such as the assidos herb, that protects against demons, and the fountain of youth.

More valuable, perhaps, than the gem-stones to be found in Prester John's empire were the small stones called nudiosi, that restored sight to the blind and improved the eyes of those whose vision was failing. A really good long stare at one of them was all that was needed to sharpen up one's vision. More fascinating, even, than the exotic land-dwelling beasts Prester John mentioned, were the fish that lived in the sea of sand, a turbulent body of sand that was fed by a river of sand and rocks. When these fish were washed up on the shore of the sandy sea, they proved to be delicious.

The Prester John letter is generally vague about geography, and, where a place is named, it is sometimes a place that the reader should not expect to find on any modern map. A region called Zone, for instance, is home to the salamanders, who can only survive in fire, and who make cocoons for themselves like silk-worms. When the salamander-silk is woven into garments, these can only be cleaned by throwing them into a fire – a medieval fantasy version of dry-cleaning. Like many such stories, the tale of the fire-resistant garments may have a germ of truth in it. In the thirteenth century, the Italian traveller Marco Polo described the asbestos clothes worn by some Mongolians, who presumably had no idea how the use of asbestos can damage human lungs. Polo was happy to confirm that asbestos was mined like coal, and was not made from the wool of an exotic lizard, as was widely believed at the time.

Like the whimsical author of the Prester John letter, whoever he or she was, John of Hildesheim combines fact, fantasy, hearsay, half-truths, misunderstandings and speculation in his *Three Kings*.

The fantastic elements John incorporates include his account of how the Kings complete a journey in thirteen days that would have taken them two years without divine aid. The author also insists on unlikely links between different parts of the Bible, so that Paul's Damascene moment comes near where Job lived, and the Three Kings meet up at Calvary, where Jesus would later be crucified. Likewise, Jesus is born near the ruined house in Bethlehem where King David was born.

John also attributes miraculous powers to people, plants and inanimate objects; so that the Three Kings can communicate without a common language, the plants in the Virgin Mary's Egyptian garden can tell if they are being tended by Christians (and wilt if they are not), and the golden crown of Melchior can heal the sick.

In giving more details about such things as the golden gifts one of the Kings gave to Jesus, the author of the *Three Kings* draws in a fanciful way on ancient classical and biblical history. The coins Melchior gives were minted by none other than Terah, the father of Abraham, and played a part in the stories of Joseph, the Queen of Sheba and others. Likewise the golden apple Melchior also gives once belonged to Alexander the Great.

In order for the Apostle Thomas to be able to meet them, the Three Kings have to live to improbably advanced ages: well over a century. Despite their personal antiquity, they are still able to endure the rigours of baptism, ordination, and elevation to the archiepiscopacy.

In John's narrative, wonders continue long after the deaths of the Three Kings. The Roman Emperor Constantine is miraculously healed of leprosy, and, although she was born two and a half centuries after the Virgin Mary left them behind, St Helen, the emperor's mother, finds Jesus' swaddling-cloths and Mary's smock fresh, whole and neatly folded when she ventures into the ruined Bethlehem house where Jesus was born.

From the start, the overall aim of the *The Three Kings* seems to be to glorify the Kings, and to give John's readers plenty of reasons to respect and admire them, and even pray to them as saints. According to John, all three of them died at advanced ages, just after celebrating Christian masses, without complaint, pain or any obvious illness. If we are to judge a man by the manner of his death, then these men were truly admirable.

John also tells us that the Kings had been ordained and elevated to the archiepiscopacy by St Thomas the Apostle, around whom many fantastic stories were assembled, partly because he was supposed to have converted many oriental groups. Prester John reminded readers of his letter that the body of Thomas lay within his empire. Miracles began to surround the bodies of the Kings even before they had all been buried, although John of Hildesheim tells us that all three died only a few days apart. As the last of them was being placed in their original tomb near the legendary Hill of Vaws, the other two 'budged up' to give him room.

As well as opening his book with a description of the universal respect accorded the Three Kings, John winds up his book with an account of how the Three Kings were remembered by various oriental churches. Here he also gives an assessment of how truly Christian, or impious and heretical, these churches are. Naturally, John favours the churches who value the Three Kings, though the author has to admit that in the east the Kings are more revered than they are in Europe.

John of Hildesheim's reason for celebrating the Three Kings is not hard to guess at. As a German monk based in a monastery that had links with both Cologne and its twelfth-century archbishop Rainard of Dassel, who escorted the relics to that city, it was an act of local patriotism for John to write in praise of the Kings. As well as giving us a glowing picture of the Kings themselves, John places them in their theological context, setting out the prophecies they fulfilled and linking them to Balaam, the Gentile prophet whom Christians believed predicted the coming of Jesus.

John's insistence on the status of the Three Kings as Gentiles is connected to his unfortunate habit of criticising the Jews, or at least defining his own version of Christianity as something opposed to their ancient faith. Although I have left some suggestions of this in the following text, I have generally removed John's anti-Semitic statements.

As well as excising most of his clueless anti-Semitism, I have removed the evidence of some of John of Hildesheim's other bad habits, in producing the following edition of the medieval English translation of his book. John tends to repeat points he has only just made, which I have usually corrected simply by deleting the repetition. It is possible that this repetition, which usually comes near the end of one of his numbered sections, has something to do with the original purpose and intended audience of the *History*. If, as the Venerable Bede did with some of his works, John of Hildesheim intended his *History* to function as something like a school textbook for novice monks, then his repetitions may have been intended as reminders of what his class had just learned.

I have also cut down some of John's long descriptions of routine matters, such as the business of hiring out horses, mules, donkeys and camels in first-century Bethlehem; and where he returns to a subject having apparently abandoned it to move on to something else, I have cut and pasted his afterthoughts so that they appear in the most logical place. In some cases, John's apparent inability to put all his thoughts on one subject in the same place (or to edit his draft text so that they do so in the final version) means that details of, for instance, the physical appearance of the Three Kings are scattered in the most unexpected places. These I have attempted to unite. I have also removed the medieval English translator's long Latin quotations and rendered his Middle English versions into modern English. I have not given the place-name 'Ind' as 'India', because John does not mean the modern state of India or anything like it: for him there were various 'Ind's in widely-separated parts of the world. I have removed John's numbering of his sections, which often correspond to places where I have introduced paragraph breaks, and I have inserted chapter headings where it seemed logical to do so.

It is hardly surprising that there exist several Middle English versions of John's work. The book was very popular in the Middle Ages, and its original Latin was translated into various languages. Some of the Middle English versions were painstakingly collated into an edition by C. Horstmann in 1886, and it is his edition that I have used for my translation into modern English.

Middle English, which should not be confused with the much older and more alien Old English or Anglo-Saxon language, was the English of the Middle Ages; the language of Chaucer, Gower, Lydgate and the anonymous Gawain poet.

It is thought that the first version of the Middle English translation Horstmann edited appeared around the time Chaucer died, i.e. *circa* 1400. Like many Middle English texts, the work of this anonymous translator uses words, usages and versions of words that the reader might wish could be returned to use in modern English. He uses 'disturbled' for 'disturbed', 'verray' for 'very' and 'gostely' for 'spiritual'. He also uses some of the letters we have lost from modern English, such as the thorn (þ) which represents the 'th' sound.

Overall, the Middle English version is lively, direct and engaging, despite the sometimes rather chaotic approach evident in John of Hildesheim's Latin original. An edited extract from the beginning of the fourteenth-century English translation is printed near the end of this book.

SW, Durham, August 2018

The Magi by Georges Trubert, French, C15th

Preface

From dusk to dawn, the whole world is full of praise for the Three Kings. In the same way that the sun rises and shines, so these Three Kings illuminate the whole world. The sun rises in the east, and the Three Kings came from the east to find and worship Christ. Christ was both a man and a god, and the Three Kings brought him gifts that were both real, and had a spiritual meaning. The Three Kings were the first sinners to believe in Christ, and in the same way that the going down of the sun is followed by its rising, so the deaths of these Three Kings were followed by the miracles that surrounded their relics.

What these Kings did at the time of the birth of Christ is well-known from books and other sources, but what they did later is not so well-known. I have therefore gathered up this information from various places and, for the glory of God and Our Lady St Mary, I have collected it together in this book.

Balaam blessing the people, Austrian, C15th

Prophecy

The story of the Three Kings begins with the prophecy of Balaam, the priest of Midian. Among other things, Balaam said that 'A star shall spring out of Jacob, and a man shall rise up out of Israel, who will be the Lord of all people' [Numbers 24:17].

Now, in the east, there are different opinions about this Balaam. In their books, the Jews say that Balaam was not a true prophet, but merely an enchanter who used witch-craft and the wiles of the devil in order to tell the future. The Christians, on the other hand, say that Balaam, who was a Pagan, was the first true prophet who was not a Jew, and that his prophecy was not aimed at the Jews, but prophesied the glorious Incarnation of Our Lord Jesus Christ and the coming of the Three Kings.

I think Balaam's prophecy cannot have come from demons, because God obviously had a hand in it. God forbade Balaam to curse the Israelites, and showed his love to Balaam by sending him an angel.

The Jews also pay Job little regard, although God Himself praised him. They say that Job was also a Pagan, who lived in Mesopotamia before the time of Moses; but the Bible itself says that Job lived in the Land of Uz, in Syria. It is thought that he lived there in a town that is now called Sabob, which is nine days' journey from Damascus. The tomb of Job can be seen there to this day. It was near the town of Sabob that St Paul was struck down, and rose up a Christian.

When the children of Israel had left Egypt behind them, and had conquered Jerusalem and the surrounding country, no man was so hardy as to oppose them in battle: everybody feared them.

In those days, there was a hill called Vaws, which was also called the Hill of Victory. This hill was the tallest in that whole region. There were always watchmen on the hill, both night and day, whose job it was to see if the army of the Israelites was advancing on the land of Ind. Later, these watchmen looked out for the approach of the Romans.

If any force was seen marching in the direction of Ind, the watchmen on the Hill of Vaws would first see the signals from the watchmen on other hills: the signals were a tower of smoke by day, and a great fire by night.

There came a time when many people in the lands of the east expected the star that was prophesied by Balaam to appear. All the great lords and the people of Ind wanted to see the star, and so they gave money and gifts to the watchmen on the Hill of Vaws, and begged them to look out for it.

They told the watchmen that if they saw any new star, that had not been in the sky before, they should immediately tell them. The watchmen of Vaws and the star that they were charged with finding became so famous throughout the east that the people of Vaws were regarded with great respect. To this day they are called the Children of Vaws, and they are celebrated and revered more than any other people in that region. The Children of Vaws are the descendants of a king called Melchior, who brought gifts of gold to our Lord Jesus Christ.

In the year 1199 the city of Acre was flourishing and virtuous. It was full of joy and prosperity, and there were many fine inhabitants, including princes and lords. There were also many Christian priests of different orders, and all manner of men from different countries, speaking all sorts of languages. In fact, the city of Acre was known throughout the world, and people from all nations came there by land and sea with merchandise to sell.

Because of the fame of Acre, and the marvels that were to be seen there, the noblest among the people called the Children of Vaws came out of Ind to the city. When they saw that everything there was even more wonderful than anything else they had seen in the east, they decided to stay. Soon they had built a strong castle there, and they brought with them from Ind many rich and wonderful ornaments and jewels. Among these was a gold crown, set with precious stones and pearls. There were characters from the Babylonian language on the crown, and a star shaped like the star that had appeared to the Three Kings. The crown was also decorated with a cross. (The banners of the Children of Vaws are still decorated with a star and a cross to this day.)

The crown had belonged to Melchior, the King of Nubia and Arabia. Thanks to the merits of the Three Kings, the crown could heal both people and animals. Even if a man was afflicted with a deadly plague, he would recover if the crown was laid on him.

Eventually this crown came into the possession of the Knight Templar, and the Knights profited greatly from the offerings that were made to it; but after the Templars were dissolved, the crown was lost, together with many other fine ornaments. This was a cause of great sorrow.

As well as the crown of Melchior and other great treasures, the princes of Vaws brought books to Acre. These were written in Hebrew and Babylonian, and they told the stories of the lives and deeds of the Three blessed Kings. Later, these books were translated into French, and it is from these books and other sources, such as sermons and homilies, that I have drawn the contents of my book.

When Hezekiah was King of the land of the Jews, Isaiah prophesied about Our Lady St Mary and her son, saying, 'A virgin shall conceive and bear a child.' [Isaiah 7:14]

In those days, King Hezekiah was sick and likely to die. Isaiah confirmed that he would die, and the King turned his face to the wall in sorrow, as it says in the Bible, not just because he feared death, but also because he had no heir. Because of this, he feared that the line of Abraham and King David would die out, and that the prophecies of Balaam and Isaiah would never be fulfilled. But Jesus Christ had mercy on Hezekiah, and prolonged his life by another fifteen years.

King Hezekiah begged God for a sign, and in response God made the sun reverse its course and go backwards in the sky. Of course the Babylonian astronomers of the time noticed this, and were astonished. When they learned that this sign had been intended for King Hezekiah, they sent him gifts and asked if they could come and worship him. But Hezekiah, out of foolish pride, pretended that the sign had nothing to do with him, and refused to thank God for it. As a result, God was angry with him, and sent Isaiah to tell the King that all the gifts the astronomers had sent him would be carried away to Babylon.

(You should understand that in those days the Babylonians and the Greeks spent a lot of time on astronomy, and took great delight in it. Among these people, even young girls knew the paths of the stars and the planets. There were well-paid masters of astronomy among the Babylonians and the Greeks, many of their men were trained up in that science, and after their training they went on to be employed by kings and princes.)

After Hezekiah, Manasseh reigned: he killed the prophet Isaiah. After Manasseh came Amon; then Josiah. In Josiah's time, Jeremiah prophesied: after Josiah came Jehoahaz, and in his time the Babylonian King Nebuchadnezzar besieged Jerusalem. Nebuchadnezzar destroyed that city, and carried off all the sacred vessels and ornaments that had been in the Temple, and in the King's palace. These the Babylonians took home with them, thus fulfilling the prophecy of Isaiah. They also brought many Jews back to Babylon as slaves.

The Bible tells us that when the Jews were in captivity in Babylon, which is fifty days' journey from Jerusalem, Jeremiah the prophet sent books of the Law of God to them so that the Law would not be forgotten.

The Babylonian captivity of the Jews was prophesied by Daniel in the time of Cyrus, King of Persia. Daniel also prophesied the incarnation of our Lord Jesus Christ, saying that, 'When He that is the holiest of saints comes, then shall your unction cease' [see Daniel 9:26].

The Babylonians translated all the books of the Jews out of Hebrew into their own language, including all the prophecies of Jeremiah, Daniel, Micah, and the other prophets. In these prophecies, including Balaam's prophecy about the star, they found that the Babylonians and the Persians often had a part to play. This made them even more fervent in their search for the star.

As well as looking out for the star from the Hill of Vaws, the people of the east looked out for the Man whose star it was: the Man who would be the Lord of all.

As I say, the Hill of Vaws is higher than any of the other hills round about. The flat top of it is so narrow that there is only space for a little chapel, which was built out of wood and stone by the Three Kings. There are stairs winding round this hill, which has many beautiful trees, herbs and spice-plants growing on its sides. Without the steps, few people would be able to climb the hill to visit the chapel, because it is so steep. Above the chapel there is a stone pillar, at the top of which is a well-made gold-plated star, which turns in the wind like a weather-vane. The light reflected from this star – sun-light by day and moon-light by night – lights up the country for a great distance. Many other marvels are told of this Hill of Vaws – so many that there is no space for them all here.

*The Emperor Augustus is told about the birth of Jesus,
German, C15th*

Bust of Augustus, Roman, marble, C1st BC

Nativity

When the time came for the Incarnation of the Son of God, Octavius was Emperor of Rome, and of the whole world, and Quirinius was the Roman Governor of Syria. The Gospel of Luke tells us that Octavius ordered a census of his Empire, which meant that every man had to go back to the place where he had been born, to be registered. Joseph, who was of the family of King David, was forced to leave Nazareth, which is a city in Galilee, to return to Bethlehem in Judea, the city of David.

Joseph took Mary his wife with him. At the time, she was heavily pregnant, and when they reached Bethlehem, she gave birth. She wrapped her new baby in cloths and laid him in a manger, because there was nowhere else to put him.

There were some shepherds in a field nearby, watching their sheep in the night. An angel of Heaven came and stood by them, glowing with a bright light. The shepherds were afraid, but the angel said, 'Do not be afraid: I bring you news of great joy for all the people. Today our Lord Christ has been born in the city of David. You will be able to recognise Him because he has been wrapped in cloths and put in a manger.'

Then, a great multitude of angels appeared, praising God and chanting 'Joy to God on high, and peace on earth to men of good will!'

Now Bethlehem never had a very great reputation, or a large population, but it has very good foundations, because beneath it there are many dens and caves. It is only two little miles from Jerusalem, and is really only a fort, but it is called a city because King David was born there. The house of Jesse, who was the father of King David, still stands in Bethlehem. In this very house, David was not only born, but also anointed as King of Israel by the prophet Samuel; and it was also here that the Son of God was born to Our Lady the Virgin Mary.

This house was at the end of a street called the Covered Street, because in order to keep off the fierce heat of the sun the street was always covered over with black cloths. Once a week in this street there was a market, where timber and second-hand clothes were sold.

When Jesus was born, all that was left of the house of Jesse was a den or cave under the earth, which was shaped like a little cellar. When there was a house standing above the cellar, the people who lived in it would use the cave below to store things – especially things that needed to be kept out of the heat of the sun.

A short time before Christ was born, the house above had been used by a man who hired out mules, horses and camels, but this house fell down. When Jesus was born there was nothing above but ruins, and a little tumbledown house in front of the cave, where bread was sold. The house was also used to store the kinds of things that were sold in the market that was held in the Covered Street, such as timber. On market-days, animals belonging to the market-traders would be tied up all round the house.

When Joseph and Mary came to Bethlehem for the census, they arrived in the city so late at night that all the beds in the city were already filled with pilgrims and other visitors. The citizens also turned Mary and Joseph away because they were dressed like poor people, and because Mary was heavily pregnant.

And so Joseph led Our Lady into this neglected house, where they found a manger set into the wall, that was about four feet long. There was a poor man's ox tied to the manger, and Joseph tied up his donkey there too. This was the same manger that Mary put her blessed son into, when she had wrapped him in cloths, because there was nowhere else to put him.

The place where the angel appeared to the shepherds on the night Christ was born is only about half a mile from Bethlehem. It was here that King David himself watched sheep when he was a child, protecting them from bears and lions. At that time of year, around Bethlehem, it would not have been very cold, and the shepherds would keep their sheep out all night, moving them from place to place in search of grazing.

It is the custom, in that part of the world, for shepherds to watch their sheep at night in the spring and autumn, when the days and nights are of equal length. In some parts of this country, where it is very mountainous in places, it is hard to tell winter from summer. In other places it is always cold, but in some places winter and summer happen at the usual times. On some of the mountains, there is snow even in August, and in some shady places in the forests, one can find snow all year round. The locals gather up the mountain snow, bring it down to the valleys, keep it in caves and sell it in the markets. The great lords of the country will buy the snow, and use it in their houses, to keep their drinks cold.

In September and October, when the sun sits low in the sky, many of the fine plants that belong to that part of the world begin to sprout and grow. Herbs and vegetables grow in March and April, and in some parts of the east corn can be harvested during those months; but usually this happens in May. It all depends on whether the land is high or low.

Around Bethlehem there is a lot of good pasture-land and fertile soil: here, for instance, barley will ripen at Christmas time, and people will send their horses and mules there for fattening at that time of the year. They put them in special stables and buy barley to feed them, and the locals call this time of year 'the time of herbs'.

At the time when Christ was born of Mary in Bethlehem, there was peace throughout the whole world.

In the days when the census was called by Augustus Caesar, Herod was made King of the Jews by the Romans. The Romans could do this because they ruled that whole area, including the lands of the Jews, Ind, Persia and Babylonia. But the people of the region all knew that Herod had no right to be King of the Jews.

The fact that Herod was King at this time fulfilled the aforementioned prophecy of Daniel, which said that God's favour would forsake the Jews after the Messiah had come. The Jews, however, continue to insist that they still have God's favour, and in those days they ignored the fact that Herod was only half-Jewish, his mother having been a Pagan.

The Christians believe that the Jews are completely confused about the meaning of the prophecy of Jacob, their Patriarch, in which he says that the sceptre of Judah shall not desert the true stock of her kings until He who has been sent shall arrive [see Genesis 49:10]. This is just one of the disputes between the Christians and the Jews of the lands of the east.

On the night when Jesus was born of Mary in Bethlehem, the twelve watchmen of the Hill of Vaws were still looking for the new star that had been prophesied by Balaam. On that very night, the star arose out of the east for the first time, shaped like an eagle and as bright as the sun. It rose into the highest part of the sky, and shone all day, so brightly that there was no difference between its brightness and the brightness of the sun when it is at its highest.

That at least is one version of the story: some books say that at the time of the Nativity of our Lord, many suns were seen, and that on the next day just one of these new suns remained in the sky. These books say that the new sun or star was unlike the paintings of the star of Bethlehem that are often seen. They say that it had many long streaks and beams, burning brighter than fire-brands, which stirred themselves about, and that in the middle of the star the shape of a young child could be seen, with a cross above him.

Some say that a voice came out of the star, saying, 'The King of the Jews is born to us this day: go, find him and worship him!'

All the people for miles around both saw and heard this star, and were amazed by it. They all knew that it was the star prophesied by Balaam, that they had waited for for so long.

Journey of the Magi, English, C12th

A Journey

At that time, the Three Kings ruled their own kingdoms in Ind, Babylon and Persia. When they were informed about the coming of the long-awaited star, they were very pleased that the star had appeared during their own life-times. The Kings lived a long way away from each other, and not one of them knew what either of the others were up to, but they all three first saw the star at the same time. All three also started to make their preparations for a journey to follow the star on the same day, and even at the same hour.

All three of them got together fine gifts and ornaments suitable for a king, and assembled long caravans of camels, mules and horses loaded with treasure. They each planned to take with them many travelling-companions, dressed up in their finest clothes, when they set off to find and worship the Lord and King of the Jews, which the voice in the star had told them to do. In fact each of the Kings took so many people with him that their caravans each looked like an army on the march. Each of the Three Kings was determined to show the greatest respect to the new King of the Jews, whom he knew would be a much greater king than he was.

Each king took with him in his caravan oxen, sheep and other beasts to eat along the way, and everything that might be needed for a long journey, including bedding, kitchen equipment and food for people and animals. So much of everything that would be needed on the journey was packed onto the mules and camels that there was plenty of everything for the whole trip, both there and back.

There were inns on the way, that provided beds and food for both travellers and their animals, but none of them could have coped with such multitudes as the Three Kings brought with them.

Because of the great heat and burning of the sun, people travel at night in the lands of Ind where the Three Kings had their homes. These eastern lands consist mostly of islands: there are great stretches of water, and also deserts, full of wild and perilous beasts and horrible serpents. There are also reeds that grow so high that men are able to make houses and ships out of them.

The islands of the east are separated by wide stretches of water, so it is very difficult to travel from one to another.

In the first of the lands of Ind was the land of Nubia, where Melchior was King at the time of the birth of Christ. Arabia is nearby, where Mount Sinai can be found, and also the Red Sea. Anyone wanting to travel from Egypt or Syria to India can easily go via the Red Sea.

Pilgrims and merchants who have sailed on the Red Sea say that the bottom is so red that all the water above it looks like red wine. The water is, notwithstanding, the same colour as any other water. It is also salty, and so clear that men can see fish and all sorts of other things on or near the bottom, even in the deepest parts.

The Red Sea has three corners, and it waxes and wanes with the tide. It is four or five miles wide: it was at the broadest place where the Children of Israel crossed with dry feet, when Pharaoh and his army chased after them and were all drowned.

A river flows out of the Red Sea into a river of Paradise, which is called the river Nile. The Nile flows through Egypt, and many fine goods come out of the east and Ind via this river. These treasures are shipped along the Nile to Egypt, Syria,

Babylon and Alexandria, and from these places they are traded all over the world.

All the soil in the part of Arabia where Mount Sinai is found is very red, and most of the stones and trees that grow there are of the same colour. There is also gold to be found there, which is also red, and grows in the rocks in the form of tiny roots. This is the best gold in the world.

There is also a mountain called Bena, where emeralds are found. It takes a lot of skill and hard work to get the emeralds out of this mountain, which is strongly guarded by servants of the Sultan.

In the second of the lands of Ind was the kingdom of Godolia, where Balthazar was the King when Christ was born: this Balthazar brought frankincense to Jesus. In ancient times, the kingdom of Sheba was in this country. Godolia has more useful species of plants than are to be found anywhere else in the east. Many of these plants produce incense, which flows out of certain trees in the form of a gum.

The third of the lands of Ind was Tarshish: Jaspar, who brought myrrh to Jesus, was King of that place. In Tarshish is an island called Egriswill, where lie the bones of St Thomas the Apostle.

There is more myrrh growing on the island of Egriswill than any other place in the world. It grows like wheat, and it looks like wheat that has been sun-burned. Myrrh grows so thick there that it sticks to people's clothes if they brush past it. In Egriswill, people take ropes and sashes and drag them through the fields of myrrh, and these are soon saturated with myrrh: it is then wrung out of them.

It was thanks to the mercy of God that the Three Kings, Melchior, Balthazar and Jaspar came from countries where there were plentiful supplies of the things they brought for Jesus. This was to fulfil the prophecy of King David, who said that the kings of Tarshish and the islands would bring gifts, as would the kings of Sheba and Arabia [see Psalm 72].

Melchior the King of Nubia, who offered gold to Jesus, was the shortest and smallest of the Three Kings. Balthazar, who offered incense, was of medium stature. Jaspar, who offered myrrh, was the biggest, and he was a black Ethiope. There can be no doubt about this, because the prophet says, 'Before him Ethiopes will fall down, and his enemies shall lick the earth. His enemies will come to him, and worship the straps of his feet.' [see Isaiah 45:14]

When each of the Three Kings had finished their splendid preparations, packed their treasures and assembled vast bands of travelling-companions, they crossed over the borders of their respective kingdoms.

We already know that they knew nothing of each other, because their kingdoms were separated by large tracts of land and sea; yet the star was so positioned in the sky that it was equidistant from each of the Kings. Because of this, each monarch and his caravan could be led by it.

Strange to say, when each of the three caravans halted, the star seemed to halt especially for them, and when they started up again, so did the star.

As we have already learned, in those days there was peace throughout the whole world, so that in every town and city they passed through, there was not a gate shut by night nor by day. Because of this, night seemed like day to the travellers, and when they passed through a city, there were people around in the streets to watch them go by. These people were astonished to see kings with vast caravans of people and animals pass through in such haste, at night. They had no idea where these kings had come from, or where they were going.

As they passed, the local people were also amazed to see how small they were, but then they remembered that the further east a person is born, the smaller, feebler and more delicate he is likely to be. Although people are smaller the closer to the rising of the sun they are born, plants and animals, particularly dangerous animals such as venomous snakes, are larger.

In the morning, the citizens of the cities through which the Three Kings passed woke to see the roads full of foot-prints and hoof-prints, and they were puzzled as to who or what could have left these marks. Some fell into debates about what it might mean.

When the Kings passed through various places, whether they were kingdoms, cities or towns, they rode over hills, through valleys and bodies of water and across plains, taking in many perilous places, without coming to any harm, or even pausing. Wherever they rode, the way seemed very plain and even to them, and it seemed that they never needed rest, food or drink; neither the people nor the animals. The whole of their journey seemed to them to take only a day, and by the mercy of God and the help of the star, the Three Kings arrived at Bethlehem at sunrise thirteen days after the birth of Jesus. (Some books say that the Three Kings reached Bethlehem in the middle of the day, travelling on dromedaries.)

There can be no doubt about the short time the Kings took, because they found Mary and her son in the same place where He was born. The fact that they arrived so quickly cannot be doubted either: as St Gregory says in a homily, the ways of God can easily be understood by anyone. This is, after all, the God who led the prophet Habakkuk from Judea to Babylon, to bring food to Daniel in the lions' den, by a hair of his head, with the speed of the wind – a distance which would usually take a hundred days for the whole trip, there and back [see Daniel 14:33-36].

This same God allowed Jesus to appear to His disciples in a house after his resurrection, though He had not passed through any gate or door. God also protected the three children who were thrown into the burning fiery furnace: in fact when they came out, they did not even smell of smoke [see Daniel 3:19-27].

The same God was able to bring the Three Kings from their

homes in the east to the Holy Land in just thirteen days, without any delays or other problems. This God, who made Mary bear a child although she always remained a pure virgin, could have brought the Three Kings out of the east into Jewry in the twinkling of an eye, as he had brought the aforementioned prophet, Habakkuk, back from Babylon. And although this God made the miraculous birth of Jesus evident to all the world, both on earth and in Heaven, through the might and majesty of his godhead, yet He took on poverty, and the frail condition of human-kind.

When these Three blessed Kings, travelling quite separately and unaware of each other, had all come within two miles of Jerusalem, a great dark cloud covered the whole earth, so that they lost sight of their star. This was prophesied by Isaiah, who said, 'Jerusalem, arise and make a light, for your light, the joy of God, has come, though darkness covers the face of the earth'. [see Isaiah 9:2]

Melchior, the King of Nubia, was ahead of the other kings, and by the will of God he arrived first at Calvary, where Christ would later be crucified. At this time, Calvary was a hill where thieves and other criminals were put to death. There Melchior rested with his company while darkness reigned, because it was so dark that he could not see his way.

Shortly after Melchior had arrived at Calvary in the darkness, King Balthazar of Godolia and Sheba arrived in the Holy Land with his retinue. He stayed near Mount Olivet, in a little town called Galilee. This town is often mentioned in holy writ, both before and after the resurrection of Christ. His disciples would meet together there in secret, for fear of the Jews. It was also in this town that Jesus appeared to his disciples after his resurrection. Galilee is also the name of a large region in that country, which is three days' journey from Jerusalem.

After Melchior and Balthazar had been in the Holy Land for a while, the dark cloud began to disperse and it was light again;

but their star was still not visible. The two Kings both saw that they were near Jerusalem, so they set out with all their followers to that city. At this time, neither Melchior nor Balthazar knew about each other at all.

Just near Calvary there is a place where three roads meet. There Melchior and Balthazar met up with Jaspar, the King of Tarshish and Egriswill. Although none of these kings had ever seen, known or even heard of the others before, they were overjoyed to see each other, and they kissed each other in gleeful greeting. Although each spoke a different language that was unknown to the others, they were nevertheless able to converse with each other.

Soon they had worked out that they were all on the same quest, and so they followed their way together with renewed determination. They soon arrived at the city of Jerusalem, just as the sun was rising. When they learned that Jerusalem was the city of the Kings of the Jews, the same one that had been besieged by the Babylonians, they rejoiced, because they thought that they would find the new-born king they sought right there.

King Herod (who was in Jerusalem at the time) and the whole city were disturbed by the sudden arrival of the Three Kings, because there were so many people and animals in their caravans that the city could not accommodate them. This recalls the prophecy of Isaiah, who said that great crowds would come to Jerusalem, with camels and dromedaries, and men from Midian, Ephah and Sheba, praising God and bringing gold and incense [see Isaiah 60:6].

When the Three Kings arrived in Jerusalem, where Herod, who was then a young man, reigned as a puppet of the Romans, they began to ask after the child they were looking for. When Herod heard about this, he gathered together all the local princes and priests and asked them where the Christ would be born. They answered, 'The prophecy says he will be born in Bethlehem, a little place, but the birthplace of a prince who will rule Israel.'

When the Three Kings made a visit to Herod, he asked them when they had first seen their star. Then he sent them away, saying, 'Go to Bethlehem and look for this child, and when you have found him, come back and tell me where he is, so that I can go there and worship him.'

The Magi approach Herod, English, C12th

An Arrival

After their visit to Herod, the Three Kings set off again, and now the star went ahead of them, leading them. They passed by the shepherds who had been visited by a bright angel, which had told them about the birth of Christ. The Kings listened to the shepherds' story with great gladness, because it confirmed what they had hoped. As the Kings and the shepherds spoke together, the star shone more and more brightly.

When the Three Kings had finished speaking to the shepherds, they gave them gifts, and set off again on their journey. As they came nearer to Bethlehem, they stopped, dismounted and dressed themselves, their followers and their animals in the very best clothes that they had. Dressed like that, the Kings in particular looked as kings should look.

As they drew nearer to Bethlehem, the star shone brighter still. At the sixth hour of the day, the Kings rode down the Covered Street, and the star came down and stood still on the ground before a little house. Soon the star flew away in a blaze of light, so that the little house and the cave were full of light. The star rose up into the heavens, and then stood still above the little house.

At last the Three Kings entered the house where Mary was with her son, and they opened their treasures and took out gold, incense and myrrh.

It is still the custom in the east for visitors to a king or sultan to have some gift of gold, silver or something else to give him. When Friars Minor visit such a man, they give him apples or pears, since they never touch gold or silver. The kings and sultans receive these gifts of fruit with great reverence and humility.

When the Three Kings visited Jesus, he was a little boy of thirteen days old. He was rather fat, and he lay on his mother's lap wrapped in rags. Our Lady was also rather fleshy, and her skin was brown in colour. In the presence of the Three Kings, she wore a poor white mantle. A linen cloth covered her whole head except for her face, and she sat on the manger. She held up Christ's head with her right hand. When the Kings had worshipped Jesus and devoutly kissed His hand, they put their gifts on one side.

The Three Kings had brought with them far greater treasures than the gifts they left with Jesus. They had rich ornaments that Alexander the Great had left behind in Ind, Babylon and Persia. They also had the treasures that the Queen of Sheba had found in Solomon's Temple, and valuables that had been looted from Jerusalem and carried off to Babylon and Persia.

When the Three Kings came into the little house and saw Jesus in the manger, wrapped in poor rags, they thought that the whole scene was so brightly lit that it was like a fiery furnace. They were so afraid that they all decided to give Jesus only the things that their hands first touched when they reached into their treasures.

Melchior reached in and found that he could only grasp a golden apple and thirty gold coins. The golden apple had once belonged to Alexander the Great. He had had it made from gold sent to him as tribute from the four corners of the earth. Alexander always carried this apple in his hand, but he left it in Ind, together with many other treasures, on his way back from the Earthly Paradise.

As soon as Melchior gave this apple to Jesus, it crumbled to dust. Jesus, who was like a pure stone cut from a mountain without the help of human hands, counted all the world and its riches as nothing, and the golden apple was broken into dust like the idol in Nebuchadnezzar's dream [see Daniel 2].

The thirty gold coins Melchior gave to Jesus had been made by Terah, the father of Abraham, in the days of Ninus, the King of Mesopotamia. They had a king's head on one side, and Babylonian letters on the other, which nobody today can read. Each one was worth about three florins.

When Abraham made a pilgrimage from Babylonia to Hebron, he used these coins to buy a plot of land for his burial and the burials of his wife, and his sons Isaac and Jacob.

When Joseph was sold by his brothers to Egyptian merchants, the merchants paid for him with these same coins. When Jacob died, the thirty coins were sent to the land of Sheba to buy spices and ointments for his burial. Eventually, the coins came into the possession of the Queen of Sheba, who offered the coins, together with many rich jewels, at the Temple in Jerusalem. Later, when Solomon's Temple was destroyed, the coins came into the possession of the King of Arabia. They passed down through the generations of kings of Arabia, until Melchior gave them to Jesus.

When the Holy Family fled to Egypt, the gifts of the Three Kings were left behind, bound up together in a cloth. These were discovered by a sickly shepherd who had tried many doctors but never found a cure for his illness. The shepherd sought out Jesus, whom he had heard of as a great healer, and Jesus healed him and taught him about the true faith. The shepherd gave Jesus the gold, myrrh and frankincense bound up in their cloth, and Jesus immediately knew what they were. He told the shepherd to offer them up at the Temple in Jerusalem. The thirty gold coins then became the coins that were given to Judas Iscariot when he betrayed Jesus.

It does say in the Gospel that Judas was given thirty *silver* coins, but as in England today, the people then did not always distinguish between different coins and different metals.

Judas became ashamed that he had betrayed Jesus, and came back to the Temple leaders to return the coins. After that, he hanged himself, and the Temple hierarchy used fifteen of the coins to buy a field in which to bury pilgrims. The other half of the money was given to the soldiers who guarded Jesus' tomb. When the coins were split up in this way, it was the first time they had been split up since the time of Abraham.

Balthazar gave a bottle of incense to Jesus because it was the first thing he felt when he reached into his treasures; likewise Jaspar's myrrh. These things the Three Kings offered with tears in their eyes.

The Kings were so aghast, and so lost in fervent devotion, that they paid very little attention to what Mary said to them. Later, they remembered that after each gift was given, she meekly bowed her head and said, '*Deo gracias.*'

*Adoration of the Magi, detail,
French or German, C14th or C15th*

A Return

When the Three Kings had thus completed their journey, given their gifts and done everything they had come to do, themselves, their followers and their animals began to eat, drink and sleep. They had, after all, not eaten, drunk or slept for thirteen days. They relaxed in Bethlehem for a while, then began to tell all the people for miles around how a wonderful star had brought them there from the farthest parts of the world.

One night, as they slept, the Three Kings were told in their dreams not to return again to Herod; and so they journeyed back to their kingdoms by a different route. On the return journey, there was no star to guide them. In fact, their star was never seen again.

The Three Kings who had met at the hill of Calvary rode home together to their kingdoms with great joy and honour. It so happened that they rode through many of the places Holofernes had ridden through with his army many years before, so that the people thought that Holofernes had returned [see the apocryphal book of Judith].

When the Kings arrived in any town or city, they were greeted reverently by the people, to whom they preached about everything they had done, seen and heard. They spoke and behaved so graciously that they were never forgotten. Although it had taken them only thirteen days to get to Bethlehem, it took each of them two years to get home. This shows how different the works of God are from the works of man.

When Herod and his scribes and the other hangers-on in his court heard that the Three Kings had gone home without coming to visit him again, Herod was very angry. Out of malice and envy he started to chase after them, but he heard nothing but praise about them from the people who had met them on their way. Herod was so annoyed to hear repeatedly about how noble the Three Kings were that he burned and destroyed all the lands the Kings had passed through. The fact that the Kings had been led by a miraculous star, and had travelled so quickly by night and day, also made Herod jealous, as well as the fact that they managed to return home without their star, with the help of guides and interpreters. In his destructive rage, Herod was particularly harsh with Sicily and Tarshish, because the people of these lands had helped the Three Kings to escape over the sea. Herod burned their ships and their goods.

After a long, hard journey, the Three Kings came to the Hill of Vaws. There they built the aforementioned beautiful chapel to honour the child they had found, and they arranged to meet up again there once a year. They also decided that they should all be buried there.

Soon all the lords, princes and knights of the kingdoms over which the Three Kings ruled heard that they were at the Hill of Vaws, and rode to meet them there. They came with great reverence, and greeted the Kings with meekness and humility. When they heard how God had worked with these Three Kings, they feared and revered them even more than they had before.

When the Kings had done everything they needed to do at the Hill of Vaws, they rode home with all their people in great joy and solemnity. But although the Kings had parted from each other, they were always together in their hearts.

At home, all three of them taught their people about what they had seen, heard and done, and in their local temples they put up stars shaped just like the one they had followed. Because of this, many Pagans turned their backs on their idols, and began to worship the child the Kings had found. And so the Three Kings lived in their own lands both piously and virtuously until the ascension of Christ, and the coming of St Thomas the Apostle.

*Simon Bening, the flight into Egypt,
Flemish, C16th*

The Flight Into Egypt

Soon after the Three Kings had started their return journey, their story, and the story of Mary and her son, began to be told everywhere. This meant that Mary and her child had to leave the little house where they were, and hide in a dark cave under the earth. They stayed there until the time came for Mary's purification. God willed it that various men and women who loved her supplied her with everything she needed to survive in hiding.

Later, when Christianity began to spread, a chapel was set up in that cave, which commemorated the Three Kings and St Nicholas. In this chapel there is a stone on which Mary used to sit to nurse the baby Jesus. Once, Mary spilled a little of her milk on this stone, and the milk can still be seen. Pilgrims often scrape some off with knives to take home as a relic, but the milk quickly re-appears.

When Mary fled to this cave, she forgot her smock and the cloths Jesus had been wrapped in. As we shall see, these were found by St Helen, the queenly mother of the Emperor Constantine, centuries later. They were still fresh and undamaged, neatly folded on top of the hay in the manger.

The time came for Mary to redeem her son at the Jerusalem Temple with an offering of two turtle doves, according to the law of Moses. There Simeon took Jesus in his arms and said, 'Now Lord, let thy servant be in peace after thy word,' and he and his wife Anne prophesied about Jesus before the scribes and the Pharisees [see Luke 2:29-32].

After this, an angel of the Lord appeared to Joseph in a dream and said, 'Arise and take the child and his mother and flee into Egypt. Stay there until I come to you again, for Herod plans to kill the child.' [see Matthew 2:13-23]

Joseph took them into Egypt under cover of night, and there they stayed for seven years, until they heard that Herod was dead.

Egypt is twelve days' journey from Bethlehem, and all along Mary's route grow the so-called roses of Jericho. They only grow along this route, and at the right time of year the shepherds of the country harvest them and sell them to pilgrims.

In the place in Egypt where Mary stayed, there is a garden that stretches as far as a man can throw a stone. Balm or balsam bushes grow in this garden, and there are seven wells there, where Mary bathed Jesus and also washed their clothes.

Balm bushes are much like rose-bushes. The ones in Mary's garden are a little over six feet high, and the leaves are shaped like trefoils. These days, each bush has assigned to it a Christian from among the Sultan's prisoners. This man's job is to tend the bush and keep it clean. There is a miracle connected to these bushes – if they are not tended by a Christian man, for instance if a Jew or a Pagan tends them, the leaves wither and refuse to grow.

During the month of March, the Sultan himself lodges in this garden, and some branches of the bushes are cut off, so that the balm bleeds out into silver bowls set under them for the purpose. The bowls are emptied into a large silver pot, which contains six gallons. This balm is for the Sultan's personal use, but if a neighbouring king requests some of it, the Sultan will send him a little vial.

When all the balm has been collected in this way, the Sultan goes home. The men who tend the bushes extract some more of the balm by boiling up the twigs and branches that were cut off to make the trees bleed. The balm is good for bruises and wounds, and it is often sold to pilgrims.

The balm extracted by boiling the twigs and branches is not as good as the balm that is collected for the Sultan. The latter type has such healing power that if just a drop of it is dropped on a man's hand, that piece of skin will never age or rot. This balm is like a thin green wine, and is called 'raw balm'. The other type is called 'sodden balm'. There is not enough space here to list all the virtues of this balm. Everyone in the east believes that the balm harvested in this garden has special powers because Mary once lived there.

After seven years, as we know, an angel told Mary and Joseph to come out of Egypt, and they went to live in the region of Galilee, in a town called Nazareth.

*Incredulity of St Thomas,
Pellegrino Tibaldi, Italian, C16th*

St Thomas the Apostle

After he had ascended into Heaven, Jesus sent His apostle Thomas to Ind to preach the Word of God. At this time, the Three Kings still reigned there. Thomas was reluctant to go, but God had decided that the same doubting Thomas who had put his fingers into Jesus' wounds should preach about the passion, resurrection and ascension of Jesus to the Three Kings. Bartholomew, Simon and Judas were also sent into Ind to preach the Word, because there are many different parts of Ind, and together they take up a very big area.

When St Thomas was travelling around the kingdoms, islands and provinces of Ind, preaching God's Word, performing miracles and healing the sick, he noticed stars displayed in all the temples. The stars had the sign of the Cross and the form of a child included in their designs, and when Thomas asked the bishops of the temples, they told him about the Hill of Vaws, and the Three Kings, and their star.

Thomas was overjoyed to hear all this, and he immediately began to teach the bishops and the people about the childhood of Jesus, his life on earth, and his passion, resurrection and ascension. He also explained to them the meaning of the Cross and the child that made up part of the design of their stars. The apostle's teaching caused many of his listeners to convert to Christianity and be baptised. He consecrated their temples, and ordered that all the idols should be removed from them.

Thomas's teaching, the miracles he performed, and the healings he accomplished, made him so famous that sick people from many miles around, and also people who were afflicted with evil spirits, came to see him. Many converted to the faith of Christ, and went on to heal people and perform miracles themselves.

After a great deal of healing and preaching, and many miracles, St Thomas arrived in the lands ruled by the Three Kings. He found them alive and well, but very old: they had all prayed that they would not die until they had been baptised. When the Kings learned that a disciple of Christ had entered their kingdoms, they dressed up in their best clothes and went to find Thomas, followed by great multitudes of their people.

Thomas received the Kings with great joy and reverence, and taught them all about Jesus. Soon the apostle had baptised the Kings, and they set about preaching the Word for themselves. As they taught the people, they told the story of how they themselves had sought Christ, and had found him in Bethlehem.

The Kings took Thomas to the Hill of Vaws along with their many followers, and the saint consecrated the chapel they had built, and preached a sermon. Thomas's fame was now so great that many pilgrims came to visit the chapel. The Three Kings built a city by the Hill of Vaws to accommodate these visitors, and it became the richest city in all the east. There Prester John lives, and the patriarch, Thomas.

Thomas the apostle ordained the Three Kings as priests, and eventually made them archbishops. As archbishops, the Kings ordained priests and bishops themselves, consecrated all the local temples to turn them into churches, and threw out the idols. The Three Kings endowed the new churches very generously, so that they could continue to grow and prosper. St Thomas taught the new priests all about the Mass, and how this sacrament began with the Last Supper. He also taught them the Lord's Prayer, and the correct way to baptise. Later, Thomas was martyred, as can be read in the book of his passion. In the country where he was killed, the people have faces like dogs, although they are not hairy like dogs.

The Magi, English, C12th

The End of the Three Kings

When the Three Kings had finished their work of Christianising their kingdoms and setting up churches, they ordered certain lords to govern their respective countries, and retired to the city they had built in the shadow of the Hill of Vaws. There they called a synod, where they instructed the people to continue in the Christian faith, and to appoint a man to replace St Thomas as their spiritual father. They suggested that this man and his successors should always be called Thomas the Patriarch.

The first Patriarch they chose was one of St Thomas's followers – a man called Jacob, who came from Antioch, and had accompanied Thomas on all his missionary journeys throughout the lands of Ind. Jacob consented to change his name to Thomas, and to this day the people of that country revere the patriarchs called Thomas just as we revere the Pope. From the time of Jacob of Antioch, these patriarchs have received a tenth of all the revenues of the kingdoms of the Three Kings.

To protect the Patriarch and his priests, and to be the temporal rather than the spiritual ruler, the Three Kings and the archbishops appointed a worthy man whom they gave the title Prester John. They gave him and his successors no other title, because nobody can rightly have a higher title than that of priest. Prester John was called John in honour of John the Evangelist, the beloved disciple of Jesus, and also John the Baptist, who baptised Jesus Himself.

When the synod had founded the line of Prester Johns and Patriarch Thomases, and ordained that men with these titles should reign in perpetuity, the members of the synod went back to their homes.

Shortly after the end of the synod, Christmas was approaching, and a new star appeared over the city by the Hill of Vaws. The Three Kings knew by this star that they were not long for this world, and so they prepared a great tomb for themselves in the city's church.

That year, the Three Kings celebrated Christmas with great solemnity, and after Melchior had said a Mass for the Feast of the Circumcision, he lay down before all the people and died, though he seemed not to have any illness. At that time, he was one hundred and sixteen years old.

The two remaining Kings had Melchior's body dressed up in his royal robes and interred in the new tomb they had made.

At the Feast of Epiphany, Balthazar died painlessly, just after saying the Mass, at the age of one hundred and twelve, and Jaspar buried him in the same tomb as Melchior. Six days later, Jaspar himself died and was buried in the same way. There was a miracle associated with the burial of Jaspar: when the people were ready to put him in the tomb, the other two Kings moved along to make space for him.

The star, which had appeared over the city just before the death of Melchior, was seen every night over the city until the bodies of the Three Kings were translated to the city of Cologne.

*St Helen with the True Cross,
workshop of Willem Vrelant, Flemish, C15th*

St Helen

After the death of the Three Kings, the Christian faith prospered in the city where they had been laid to rest, until the Devil and his wicked angels began to promote various heretical opinions among the people.

However hard they tried, neither Prester John nor Patriarch Thomas could turn the people away from their folly, and inevitably they fell into their old habits again, and began to worship idols and false gods. They forsook the Law of the one true God, and neglected to show the bodies of the Three Kings the proper respect. In fact they almost forgot that the Three Kings were buried in their city at all, and so people from the Kings' original kingdoms came and took the bodies away, having first respectfully sealed them up in chests. These bodies were received with great reverence in their own countries, and remained among their own people for many years.

Thanks to the miracles of God, the Roman Emperor Constantine was healed of his leprosy and converted to Christianity by St Silvester. The Law of Christ changed him to a new man, and at the same time his mother Helen became a Christian, as can be read in the story of the finding of the True Cross.

Before her conversion, Queen Helen had been a bitter enemy of Christianity, but when she turned to Christ she became the greatest preacher of God's Word in the whole country where she was living. Out of devotion to Jesus and his mother Mary, she also diligently sought out the places in the Holy Land which Christ had hallowed with his presence. She visited Calvary, where Jesus was hung on the Cross, and where he committed his mother to the care of St John the Evangelist. She also visited the place where Christ was laid in the tomb, where he had also appeared to Mary Magdalene in the guise of a gardener. At these and many other holy places, Queen Helen set up royal churches. She also set up churches in Nazareth and in less well-known places, and also established and endowed archbishops, bishops, priests and other ministers to serve in them.

At the place where the angel had appeared to the shepherds, she set up a church which she called the Gloria in Excelsis church. This church still bears that name, and was once a great college of canons.

In Bethlehem, Helen found the dark little house where Christ had been born. Nobody had set foot in the place since that time, and, as we know, Helen found the hay and the manger Christ had been laid in, the cloths he had been wrapped in, and Mary's smock, all whole and free of any decay. These the queen took back to Constantinople and set up in the city's church of St Sophia.

The relics Helen had found in Bethlehem remained in Constantinople until the time of the French King Charles, who travelled to Jerusalem to fight the Saracens, and freed many Christian prisoners. He returned home via Constantinople, and begged to be allowed to take the relics with him. These he placed in the church at Aachen, where they remain to this day.

After she had done these wonderful things in the Holy Land, St Helen turned her thoughts to the bodies of the Three Kings, and set off for the land of Ind. There she continued to preach and set up churches, and renewed the Christian faith of the people, who had been converted by St Thomas, but had fallen into the aforementioned heresies. The stories about St Helen – how she had found the True Cross for instance – brought many people to listen to her.

It took St Helen a long time to obtain the bodies of two of the Three Kings: Melchior and Balthazar. In this, she was aided by Prester John and Thomas the Patriarch. Jaspar's body was on the island of Egriswill, where it was in the possession of the Nestorians. St Helen persuaded these heretics to give her Jaspar's body in return for the body of St Thomas the Apostle, which she happened to have with her at the time.

According to a local prophecy, the body of Thomas the Apostle will eventually end up in Cologne, during the time of a future archbishop of that city, who will be so wise and powerful that he will arrange a marriage between the son of the Roman Emperor and the daughter of the Emperor of Tartary. When this marriage has been contracted, the Holy Land will be in Christian hands. Because they expect to lose it eventually, the Nestorians of Egriswill pay very little attention to Thomas's body.

When the bodies of the Three Kings were at last reunited, a lovely perfume emanated from them, which sweetened the country for miles around. St Helen put the bodies together in one beautiful, elaborate chest, and brought them to Constantinople in a joyous procession.

The Three Kings were installed in the Church of St Sophia in Constantinople. Constantine himself, with the help of a little boy, had set up all the marble pillars in that church, which at one time had the Crown of Thorns among its treasures. The Crown of Thorns was given by a later emperor to a king of France who had helped him fight the Turks and Saracens.

Once the Three Kings were installed in St Sophia, people came from miles around to visit them and worship them, and many miracles happened at their shrine.

The Magi, German, C13th

More Travels

After Constantine and his mother Helen had died, more heresies began to appear in the Christian Church, and some of the faithful were killed just for following the true Law of Christ. Although they had many learned bishops among them, the Greeks broke off from the true Church and chose their own Patriarch. They continue to follow this Patriarch to this day, as we follow the Pope.

At this time, the bodies of the Three Kings were not respected by the Greeks, and many Christian lands, including Armenia, were lost to the Saracens and the Turks. With the help of the city of Milan, the Emperor Maurice regained these lands, and in gratitude he gave Milan the bodies of the Three Kings.

There is also a story that a Greek Emperor called Manuel gave the bodies of the Three Kings to a wise and holy man called Eustorgius to take to Milan. There they were laid to rest in a fair church, and many miracles were witnessed at their shrine.

Later, the city of Milan began to rebel against the Emperor Frederick. Frederick called on Rainald, the Archbishop of Cologne, for help. With the assistance of various local lords, Rainald captured Milan and demolished most of the city. Before this happened, some of the leading Milanese had buried the Three Kings in the earth to hide them; but a Milanese lord called Asso asked Rainald to come to him where he was held as a prisoner of war, and told the Archbishop the location, to win the favour of his bitter enemy, Frederick.

Asso was released and brought the bodies to Rainald, who

in turn begged Frederick to allow him to take them to Cologne. Frederick assented, and the Archbishop brought them in a grand procession. At Cologne, the bodies were interred in the Cathedral of St Peter, to the great joy of the citizens. Even now, people from all the nations visit the Three Kings at Cologne, and miracles are attested there every day.

Adoration of the Magi,
Defendente Ferrari, Italian, c. 1520

Devotion

Prester John, the lord of the land of Ind, and all the kings that rule under him, go to church and hear mass on the twelfth day after Christmas, which we call the Feast of Epiphany. For this occasion, Prester John and the kings dress themselves as kings should be dressed, with crowns on their heads and many rich ornaments.

People belonging to many of the different Christian sects in the East have a special reverence for the Three Kings. They fast on Christmas Eve, and on Christmas Day they set out enough food and drink to last them until Twelfth Night. They also set up a candle by all this food, which burns through that whole time. Then there is great joy and mirth for all the family, and at the Feast of Epiphany people set off to visit their friends and neighbours with candles in their hands, and they eat, drink and dance all night.

The candles they carry at this time stand in for the star of Bethlehem, and the way the people turn night into day reminds them of how the star of Bethlehem once made night as light as day.

On Twelfth Night many Christians from all the different sects make a pilgrimage to the River Jordan, which is five miles from Jerusalem. They go with their bishops, abbots, priests and others carrying silver crosses and censers, and when they get to the river they lay their crosses on the ground and read from the Gospel about the Three Kings. They then offer fervent prayers to their crosses, to remember the Three Kings, who offered gifts to Jesus.

After this, the pilgrims process to the place where Christ was baptised by John the Baptist, and there they also read out the relevant part of the Gospel. They then bless the river water and wash their crosses in it. After this, sick and blind men go into the water naked, and come out cured. When all this has been accomplished, the pilgrims return to their own countries.

Christians in the east who live too far from the River Jordan go to their nearest river to perform these ceremonies. On the journey, they enjoy a kind of apple called an 'orange', which ripens at this time of year.

Between the River Jordan and Jerusalem is the desert where John the Baptist lived and preached, and where Jesus came to be baptised by John. Also in this desert, Jesus fasted for forty days and forty nights.

Many Christians who live in the places the Three Kings passed through have a special reverence for the Kings. Even the Saracens, who live under the Law of Muhammed, revere them. Some of their mosques were once Christian churches, and though the Muslims have defaced many of the statues by cutting off their noses and poking their eyes out with knives, they always leave the statues of the Three Kings alone.

The Nubian Christians live in the lands of Arabia and Nubia, where Melchior was once King, and they are true Christian men. Their priests wear gold or gilt crowns when they serve at the altar, in memory of the Three Kings.

There is also another sect called the Soldini, who live in the Kingdoms of Godolia and Sheba, which were once ruled by Balthazar. Their faith is somewhat corrupt, and they have named themselves after a heretic called Soldinus, so their sect is not so well-respected as that of the Nubian Christians. When their priests approach the altar to celebrate Mass, they carry gold, incense and myrrh with them, which they do in memory of the Three Kings and their gifts.

In the Kingdom of Tarshish, and on the Island of Egriswill, where Jaspar once ruled, there is a sect called the Nestorians: they are named after a heretic called Nestorius. They do not follow the faith or Law of the Holy Church, and they do not reverence or worship the Three Kings. Really, they are the worst of the heretics, and they have infested and corrupted forty different countries. All the other sects hate them and their priests. They broke away from Prester John and Thomas the Patriarch, and no amount of preaching or teaching from the best authorities can bring them to their senses.

It was the will of God that there should be an uprising against the Nestorian rulers of certain countries, and a great multitude of people, including shepherds, labourers and slaves, made a blacksmith their leader and started a rebellion. These rebels, who called themselves Tartars, destroyed the kingdoms of the Nestorians and killed all the people, both old and young, without mercy. They took over all the Nestorian castles and cities, and they live in them to this day.

When the Tartars had overrun them, the Nestorians appealed to Prester John and promised to return to the old, true Christian Way if only he would come to their aid. Prester John thought that he might help them, but the Three Kings appeared to him in a dream and told him that he should give no succour to the Nestorians. 'It is God's will,' said the Three Kings, 'that they should be utterly destroyed, because of their malice and their wickedness.'

When Prester John had told them about his dream of the Three Kings, the Nestorians approached all the greatest men of Prester John's court, and gave them rich gifts in the hope that they would persuade Prester John to help them. As a result, several of his great lords counselled Prester John that he should take no heed of dreams or visions, but should return to his first purpose, which was to help the Nestorians.

And so Prester John sent his oldest son, who was called David, at the head of a great army to help the Nestorians. But when David's army and the Tartar army met together in battle, the Tartars won, and killed David and all his host. Not a single soldier escaped, and the victorious Tartars went on to lay waste to many lands, castles and cities that belonged to Prester John.

When Prester John heard about all this destruction, he regretted going against the advice of the Three Kings, who had appeared to him in his dream. In great sorrow of heart he prayed for the mercy, help and grace of God and the Three Kings.

Today, there are very few Nestorians left. They no longer have their own kingdoms, and are forced to pay tribute to live in other people's countries.

Later, the Three Kings appeared to the Emperor of Tartary in a dream, and told him not to do any more harm to Prester John. They told him to make a lasting peace with him, but to keep the castles and cities he had won from him, 'because,' they explained, 'he did not do as we told him.'

Although he was a Pagan, the Emperor of Tartary was deeply impressed by his vision, and he lost no time in sending peace envoys to Prester John. They agreed to a lasting peace, and from that day their families have inter-married, the eldest daughter of one of them always marrying the eldest son of the other.

The Emperor of Tartary was curious about the Three Kings who had appeared to him, and when he had learned their story, he decided that all the first sons of his successors should be named Jaspar, Balthazar or Melchior.

Prester John's own country has not been free of sects. The sect that has taken root there is, however, a truly Christian one. In memory of the Three Kings, they hang golden crowns over their altars, and three priests approach the altar from three different directions to perform the Mass. This they do in remembrance of the way that the Three Kings came together at the place where their three roads met.

Another eastern sect, that of the Syrian Christians, has little heresy in it. They greatly honour St Barbara, and keep vigil all night at the time of her feast. At that time, they give all their neighbours presents of seeds, which are later sown in their gardens. When the Syrian Christians swear to tell the truth before a magistrate, they always swear on the Gospel and the Three Kings.

There is another sect, called the Maronites, the priests of which have wives. They are widely scattered, and they never say Mass except at Christmas and Easter. In these masses, they honour St Thomas and the Three Kings.

The sect of the Nicholaites give alms daily to poor people, to honour God and the Three Kings.

There are so many sects that have a special devotion to the Three Kings that there is not room for a full account of them all here. The fact is that in the East, especially in the lands where the Three Kings were once the rulers, the people generally revere the Kings more than Christians do in Europe.

And Jesus Christ continues to perform many miracles in the countries of the East because of the merits and prayers of these holy Kings, who now reign in the high bliss of Heaven. To which bliss I hope He who reigns above the kings and saints will bring us all. Amen.

Herod and his soldiers, English, C12th

The Opening of the Book in Middle English

Sithe of þese þree worschipfull kynges alle þe worlde from þe risyng of þe sonne to his downe-goynge ys full of preisyng and merites and, þerfore, as the rysyng of þe son clerith in hys beemes, so þis world shyneth in meritis of þese þree kyngis; ffor in þe springyng and rysyng of þe sonne, þat is to saye in þe Este of þe worlde, these þree kynges in body and flessh lyuynge, Crist, verray god and man, wiþ her ʒiftis, þat were bodily & in menynge gostely, sought and worschiped, and so þese þree kynges, þat of myscreauntes were þe first byleuyng men and of myscreauntes þe firste maydenes, þe birth of Crist, þe verray sonne, fyrste schewed and honoured amonge mysbeleued men and so goynge-doune of þis sonne in þe bileue of þese þree kyngis, as a shynyng morowetyde bitokeneth a cleer wheder folowing.

The Wise Men, from Matthew Chapter 2, World English Bible (Matt 2:1-12)

Now when Jesus was born in Bethlehem of Judea in the days of King Herod, behold, wise men from the east came to Jerusalem, saying, "Where is he who is born King of the Jews? For we saw his star in the east, and have come to worship him." When King Herod heard it, he was troubled, and all Jerusalem with him. Gathering together all the chief priests and scribes of the people, he asked them where the Christ would be born. They said to him, "In Bethlehem of Judea, for this is written through the prophet,

> 'You Bethlehem, land of Judah,
> are in no way least among the princes of Judah:
> for out of you shall come a governor,
> who shall shepherd my people, Israel.'"

Then Herod secretly called the wise men, and learned from them exactly what time the star appeared. He sent them to Bethlehem, and said, "Go and search diligently for the young child. When you have found him, bring me word, so that I also may come and worship him."

They, having heard the king, went their way; and behold, the star, which they saw in the east, went before them, until it came and stood over where the young child was. When they saw the star, they rejoiced with exceedingly great joy. They came into the house and saw the young child with Mary, his mother, and they fell down and worshipped him. Opening their treasures, they offered to him gifts: gold, frankincense, and myrrh. Being warned in a dream that they shouldn't return to Herod, they went back to their own country another way.

Bibliography

Baring-Gould, Sabine: *Curious Myths of the Middle Ages*, Sagwan, 2018

Brown, Raymond E.: *The Birth of the Messiah*, Geoffrey Chapman, 1993

Horstmann, C. (ed.): *The Three Kings of Cologne*, Trubner, 1886

Longenecker, Dwight: *Mystery of the Three Kings*, Regnery, 2017

Molnar, Michael R.: *The Star of Bethlehem*, Rutgers University Press, 2013

Munz, Peter: *Frederick Barbarossa*, Eyre & Spottiswoode, 1969

For free downloads and more from the Langley Press,
please visit our website at:

http://tinyurl.com/lpdirect